CAREER PATH RESUSCITATION (CPR)

FORGE A NEW CAREER PATH, WORK WHEREVER YOU WANT & LIVE LIFE ON YOUR TERMS

MICHELLE KULP

Copyright © 2020 by **Monarch Crown Publishing**

All Rights Reserved. No part of this book may be
reproduced in any form without permission in writing from the author.
Reviewers may quote brief passages in reviews.
ISBN: 978-1-7340538-9-0

This book is designed to provide accurate and authoritative information in regard to the subject matter herein. It is sold with the understanding that the author and publisher is not engaged in rendering legal, accounting, or other professional services. If you require legal advice or other expert assistance, you should seek the services of a competent professional.

While the author has made every effort to provide accurate website addresses and other information at the time of publication, neither the publisher nor the author assumes any responsibility for errors or changes that occur after publication. Further, the publisher does not have any control over and does not assume any responsibility for author or third-party websites or their content.

"It is far better for a man to go wrong in freedom than to go right in chains."
— **Thomas H. Huxley, English biologist;
known as "Darwin's Bulldog"**

"Become the architect of your career by considering your desired career path, location, salary, scope, organization type, benefits and perks, and mentors… *Be a brand, not an employee.*"
— **Kanika Tolver, author of *Career Rehab***

"To find the best job in the world, sometimes you have to create it yourself."
—**Jeff Taylor, founder and CEO of Monster.com**

"Middle managers and corporate wage slaves don't appear to be winning. Their skills are less in demand and more likely to be automated, contracted, or outsourced. Maybe their hanging on to the final dangling remnants of the ladder they were climbing or clinging anxiously to the full-time corporate job they've managed to hold on to so far. Their income is stagnating, their benefits are shrinking, and they are too slowly coming to terms with the reality that they no longer have job security. These workers are surviving in their full-time jobs, but struggling if they lose them."
— **Diane Mulcahy, author of *The Gig Economy***

"My father had one job in his lifetime, I will have six jobs in my lifetime, and my children will have six jobs at the same tim*e*."
— **Robin Chaser, Founder of ZipCar**

"If you're like most Americans, you will spend around five years of your life engaged in some type of job search activity. You'll hold about eleven different positions in the course of your career, and each job search might take you six months or longer. The new normal is not only to switch jobs but to change professions – which isn't easy to accomplish. When you want to make a 180-degree change, you need a savvy understanding of the art and science of the job search."
— **Dawn Graham, author of** *Switchers:*
How Smart Professionals Change Careers and Seize Success

"You can't model for the rest of your life,
so it is important to diversify your career."
— **Tyra Banks**

"This is the beginning of anything you want."
— **Anonymous**

Table of Contents

Introduction 1

My Story 5

Chapter 1: Breaking Bad Career Path Habits 11

Chapter 2: Reflect 17

Chapter 3: Re-Vision 25

Chapter 4: Renew 37

Chapter 5: Reposition 47

Chapter 6: Repackage 63

Chapter 7: Re-Purpose 75

Chapter 8: Closing Thoughts 87

Introduction

COVID-19 is disrupting not only how we work, but if we work at all.

- Did your job suddenly disappear?
- Have you been replaced by outsourcing or technology?
- Has COVID-19 completely disrupted your industry?
- Are you worried about your financial future because of your job status?

The New York Times reported that COVID-19 pushed more than 16 million Americans out of work in less than one month.

Almost every industry has been affected by this pandemic in some way. Some industries, such as airlines, travel, retail, marketplaces, restaurants, tourism, sports, entertainment, health services, speakers, cruise lines, and real estate, have seen a significant impact.

If you find yourself in a **CAREER PATH EMERGENCY**, I have good news – there is a *HIDDEN OPPORTUNITY* for you to create a brand NEW Career Path. You can breathe new life into a dead-end career path, but only if you act swiftly.

Despite the depressing news, I believe this could be an extraordinary opportunity for you to adjust your career path. When you step back and reflect, you may find that you were operating in default mode rather than creation mode. Consider these two questions:

1. Am I (or was I) on the career path I truly wanted to be on at this point in my life?
2. Is there a gap between the career path I was on and my dreams?

Before COVID-19, there was already a massive shift taking place in the job market due to a phenomenon known as the "long term leak in job creation." As a result, "businesses have been starting in fewer numbers, with fewer employees, growing slower, and therefore, generating increasingly fewer new jobs for the U.S. Job market."

Additionally, many companies were already eliminating full-time jobs through layoffs, downsizing, and reorganization. Instead of hiring full-time employees with benefits, companies are breaking jobs down into smaller projects or tasks that can be automated or outsourced. By doing so, these companies are more flexible, lean, profitable, and efficient.

Recently, this article appeared in my Google newsfeed:

"Walmart says it is removing cashiers and standard conveyor belt lines at one of its popular superstores…it says it is an attempt to see if checkout times are faster while limiting human interaction in the age of the coronavirus… Depending on the success of the test run, Walmart could expand the program to more stores."

The full-time employee is rapidly disappearing as companies increase outsourcing tasks to independent contractors. For example, a company can fill a vacancy for a full-time marketing manager with a few subcontractors such as a copywriter, social media manager, and public relations expert. Paying only for work when needed saves the company time and money.

In his book, "The End of Jobs," author Taylor Pearson says:

"Today, a $40 internet connection and a free Skype account gives anyone access to the greatest talent pool in history. Instead of competing against the labor pool of a few hundred thousand or a few million people in your area near you for your job, you're competing against seven billion people around the world."

Platforms like Upwork, Elance, Freelancer, and others now make it possible to hire and manage subcontractors worldwide.

The end of jobs has been accelerated due to COVID-19.

The world is changing at lightning speed, and we must adapt quickly or get struck down by this powerful storm.

Taylor Pearson says that many of us are asking the wrong question:

"The problem both as a society and as individuals is that we're asking the wrong question:
How do I get a job doing that?
What if the better question is:
"How do I create a job doing that?"

You have the power right now to create and design a career path that is better aligned to your schedule, passions, unique skill set, and needs.

It's important to know that COVID-19 is not solely to blame for these job market changes; globalization and technology are contributing factors as well.

Moreover, many companies will no longer require employees to work in a physical building at a specific location.

A family member of mine who works for a large cable company told me that his company moved an entire customer support department with thousands of employees in multiple states to working remotely from home within a few weeks.

Even before the COVID-19 lockdown ends, companies are rethinking whether they need to lease office space in expensive metropolitan areas, when they can operate at greater efficiency with a virtual team.

> *If you want to go from location-stuck to location-independent, from trapped in a corporate schedule to working your own hours, and from a limited paycheck to writing your own paycheck, you are in the right place.*

It takes a little re-framing of the status quo to see what enormous opportunities you have right now.

Freedom is literally at your fingertips.

You owe it to yourself to create a career and life that meets *your* needs. The time is now for you to make this shift quickly.

This book will give you the tools you need to create the career of your dreams.

Let's get started!

My Story

Hi! My name is Michelle Kulp, and I spent 17 years in the legal field working as a Paralegal. I loved my career for over a decade, and then I experienced *Career Creep*. The job I once loved slowly shifted over time until I was no longer doing what I loved. I felt like a cog in the wheel of a big, well-oiled corporate machine, and I lacked *fulfillment, freedom,* and *flexibility*.

Luckily in 2000, the 600-person law firm I worked at restructured my department, and I was given a pink slip. I was a single mom of three young children and had no idea what else I would do to pay the bills. At the time, I was living paycheck-to-paycheck.

My dream was to be a full-time writer, but I didn't know how to quickly make a career path move and still enjoy the same or similar compensation and benefits I had in the legal field.

I received a small amount of severance pay, so I had a little time to think about what I wanted to do. I decided I would become a full-time reporter for the local newspaper. Since I had no experience and no credentials, like a "journalism degree," I decided to *fake it* until I could *make it*. I literally pretended to be a reporter and attended local events, interviewed people, took pictures, and wrote articles.

My father, who was a local government employee, would see the editor of the newspaper every day while he was walking to work. One day, I gave my father a gold envelope with my story and photos in it and asked him to give it to the editor when he saw him on his way to work in the morning.

Within a week, my first article was published on the front page of the local newspaper! I was ecstatic and thought, "My dream is coming true!" This went on for about a month with four articles published (without compensation) until the editor of the newspaper finally called me and said, *"What do you want a job or something?"*

I asked him if he was offering, and he said, "Come to my office and talk to me."

I went to his office the very next day thinking I would be hired as a reporter and my dream of becoming a full-time writer would come true.

I was close…

As I entered his office, the editor asked me to shut the door behind me and said, "You see those reporters out there? Well, I have to do a lot of editing when they turn in stories. But I didn't have to edit the stories you turned in over the last few weeks. You have a real gift, and I want to offer you a full-time job as one of my reporters."

OMG?! What?! I couldn't believe that he was offering me my dream job!

There was one BIG problem…

The salary I was offered was $25K. I told him I was earning $50K as a Paralegal, and he said that, unfortunately, $25K was the going rate.

There was no way I could accept my "dream job" because I would not have been able to pay my bills or take care of my three young children.

Luckily, he allowed me to be a freelance writer for the next few years, and that gave me a lot of experience, confidence, and freedom.

It was also my introduction to the world of freelancing and creating multiple streams of income.

For the next few years, I created multiple streams of income, and I loved it this new way of working!

Then, I read a book by Barbara Stanny, called *Secrets of Six-Figure Women* and decided I needed to make six figures.

I didn't focus on the *how*. I just set my intention that I would make six figures "doing what I loved."

Within a short time, I responded to an ad in the *Washington Post* that read "Sales Professional Wanted. Sell a fun product. Make 6 figures. Work 20 hours. Play Golf."

I didn't really care about golf, but I saw the magic words, "Make 6 figures" and "Work 20 hours."

I called the phone number listed on the ad, and when they answered, I said, "Hello, my name is Michelle Kulp, and I'm you're next top sales rep!"

The gentleman on the other end of the phone was taken aback and asked, "Really? And exactly what type of in-home, one-call close experience do you have?"

I had no idea what a "one-call close" was, but as a teenager, I worked in my dad's retail store, Bond's Clothing—a men's suit store. So, I convinced him I had *some* sales experience, and he finally gave in and asked me to fax him my resume.

Since I had very little sales experience on my resume, I had to be creative. Anything I ever did that was remotely related to sales went on this new (made-up) resume. Then, I typed a list of the ***"Top 10 Reasons Why **** Should Hire Me,"*** and faxed it to the hiring manager with my new resume.

I learned that 200 applications were submitted for the job, and they narrowed it down to 20 candidates. To my surprise, I was one of the top 20 selected. I was so excited and didn't give much thought to the product I would be selling; I just cared about making six figures and working only 20 hours a week.

I competed with 20 men who had many years of outside "one-call close" experience. During the interview, I was asked why I would make a good salesperson. My response was:

"I'm a warm and caring person. If I have a great product to sell, backed by an outstanding company, people will warm up to me and buy the product."

They thanked me for my time, and I went home.

I truly believed I would not be offered the job because I lacked the experience they desired. Also, I didn't know the sales lingo, and I felt like I was in way over my head.

The very next day, the hiring manager called and offered me the job. I couldn't believe it. I was jumping for joy. I accepted the position (by the way, it was 100% commission), and before we hung up, I said, "Do you mind if I ask you a question? You interviewed so many applicants who had a lot more experience than me. Why did you hire me without that experience?"

He said, "We hired you because you have NO bad habits."

Wow! He later told me that he didn't like hiring salespeople who had a lot of experience because it was hard for them to "unlearn" what they knew about sales. This company had a specific format to follow in order to be successful. Since I didn't know anything about in-home sales, they felt I could easily be trained in their system and become a great salesperson.

They were right; I became one of the top 10% income earners in the company. I worked in that all-commission job, 20 hours per week, earning six figures per year for about ten years until the company filed bankruptcy due to the real estate crash.

I am thankful for this company and the experience and knowledge I received while working there.

Once I began making six figures working part-time in outside sales, I decided to start an online business, www.becomea6figurewoman.com, in 2005.

Over the years, I made money online (while working my sales job which gave me a lot of freedom and flexibility) in various ways such as copywriting, ghostwriting, website design, SEO, royalties from writing books, coaching, and selling online courses. Now, I make multiple six figures from www.bestsellingauthorprogram.com.

I took many of the skills I already possessed and used them in new ways. I also learned new skills and was able to do something I call "skill stacking," which I'll talk about more in an upcoming chapter.

I want you to have the same freedoms as I have – time and money freedom.

It pains me to see so many people struggling to make ends meet, feeling powerless, and under a lot of stress because they don't know how to take the equity they've already built in their jobs and transfer that over to a new career path in a new way.

I am writing this book to show you that you are *not* powerless. You can and must shift your career path now, especially if you are unemployed, underemployed, or unhappy in your current situation.

Let's get started. Chapter One will show you how to remove your old career path habits and create new ones that are more in alignment with who you are and the *NEW WORLD* in which we live.

Chapter 1: Breaking Bad Career Path Habits

Sometimes the world shifts slowly, and sometimes it shifts rapidly. COVID-19 is changing the job market by leaps and bounds.

This chapter is about breaking the status quo of how we think about jobs; without a doubt, a major paradigm shift is needed.

Every generation is raised to think differently about jobs and careers. For example, Millennials don't typically stay in one job for very long and are content with working multiple freelance jobs. Baby boomers, however, were raised to believe you should have one job for your entire career before you retire.

As the job market and the world changes, we need to change our outdated Career Path Habits. See which habits you can relate to from the list below.

Outdated Career Path Habits

1. Get a job and stay with the same company for the rest of your career; even if you hate it, it's not fulfilling, and it's causing you stress and anxiety. Suck it up.
2. Depend on one stream of income to pay all of your living expenses.
3. Stay in one industry or one career forever; loyalty at all costs.
4. Powerless to change careers and feel like you are starting all over again if you make a career path move.
5. Putting your job ahead of your health, family, relationships, and dreams.

6. You have no passion for what you do, but it pays the bills, so you stay.
7. You've only had one type of job or career path, and you stay in it because you don't know what else you could do.
8. You believe you have job security.
9. You have too much debt and a certain lifestyle, so you can't change careers. You may even have a mortgage that keeps you stuck in an undesirable job.
10. You don't understand how to transition from one career path to another.

As you read in my story above, I had many of these limited and outdated career path habits. If I had not been fired from the law firm, it's sad to say, but I would probably still be working there because my decisions were based on my survival. I didn't have the courage to change career paths; thankfully, the law firm helped me out by firing me. I knew deep down that I wasn't happy, so once they let me go, I decided I would do whatever it took NOT to go back there!

Now, let's look at the new, updated career path habits for the modern world in which live.

Updated Career Path Habits for the Post COVID-19 Job Market

1. Be a brand, not an employee.
2. Don't expect security from one job. Expect to hold multiple positions throughout your career and have a variety of diverse work experiences. Job security is a myth.
3. Diversifying creates security. Create income security by creating multiple streams of income.
4. Stop trading time for money and start creating value.

5. The Gig Economy is here to stay.
6. Stop looking for a job, and create a more aligned and satisfying career that helps you achieve your vision of professional and personal success.
7. Have an opportunity mindset (instead of an employee mindset) to learn on the job, at your own pace, and in lower-risk situations.
8. Think access, not ownership. Keep your fixed costs low so you can easily adjust to changes in your earnings.
9. Schedule time off and vacations frequently.
10. Always be learning. Learners are earners.

Can you feel the freedom, flexibility, and fulfillment radiating out of the updated Career Path Habits?

In *The Wizard of Oz*, Dorothy discovered at the end of the movie that she always had the power to go home. In the new world we live in, you have the power to create a life you love! The COVID-19 crisis has interrupted and disrupted life as we know it but has also given you the gift of having a new perspective. Forced change is not always pleasant (*anything unplanned is rarely pleasant or welcome*), but it is necessary to restructure the status quo.

Many of us have CAREER PATH TUNNEL VISION, which has left us in the same career spot for a long time. When we do not see changes, our response is to work harder, which is not the answer. Changing, adapting, and removing our blinders of denial will allow us to see the different paths available.

In the upcoming chapters, we will focus on the six "R's" of Career Path Resuscitation:

- **Reflection** – Assessing where you've been so you can identify your JOB EQUITY in four main areas to create something new.
- **Revision** – Creating a new vision for your life and your career path.
- **Renew** – Renewing your priorities, values, and commitment to yourself.
- **Reposition** – Repositioning yourself from an employee to a brand.
- **Repackage** – Repackaging your skills and the value you bring to the world.
- **Repurpose** – Discovering your *new* purpose.

I admit, when I was utterly miserable working at the law firm, I was a CAREER PATH WIMP. I didn't have the courage to quit my job even though I was physically, mentally, emotionally, and spiritually drained. I believe that being fired was nature's way of telling me that I was in the wrong job/career path.

I thought my legal career would last forever; it was hard for me to accept that my passions and priorities had changed. I had to let go of my identity as a paralegal, which at the time I considered was my entire identity. Who was I now that I didn't have a career, title, salary, hours, office, benefits, and social life? I felt like I no longer had an identity, and it was scary.

Imagine how an artist feels when they look at a blank canvas or how a writer feels seeing a blank page.

It is scary, but it's also exhilarating. You GET TO create and design a life you love – one that provides *fulfillment, freedom,* and *flexibility.* I believe we all have these three innate desires, but we repress them and forget about them over the years. We've been accustomed to job misery.

Let's get started on this exciting new career path journey...

Chapter 2: Reflect

*"Life can only be understood backward,
but it must be lived forward."*
— Soren Kierkegaard

In this chapter, we are going to harness the power of hindsight.

In my book, "Quit Your Job and Follow Your Dreams," I talk about performing a job autopsy. The job autopsy tool was designed to help you look back at the tasks you performed in each of your jobs and rate them to see what brings you alive and what sucks the energy out of you.

We are going to use a new tool as we take a trip down Career Memory Lane to identify the "equity" you've built up in your past jobs.

In the book, "Love It Don't Leave It: 26 Ways to Get What You Want at Work," authors Beverly Kaye and Sharon Jordan-Evans explain more about job *equity*:

"The longer we stay with a job, the more we built some unique forms of equity. Consider the equity you've built in your current job:

- **Skill Equity**: The knowledge, the know-how that you've developed over time. The special capabilities and competencies that bring you respect for a job well done and enable others to count on you.

- **Social Equity**: The friends and colleagues you've gotten to know (they often feel like family) or the customers you enjoy interacting with.

- **Influence Equity**: The ability to get your ideas heard, the connections you've learned to use, the resources that others make available to you so you can get your job done.
- **Financial Equity**: The dollars you get for the job you do plus the retirement, investment, or bonus funds, insurance, memberships (even perks such as a parking space), all in return for your know-how and commitment."

Let's begin with *Skill Equity*. For each job you've had, list the skills you developed and mastered at that job. Fill out each of the boxes to create more clarity around that skill.

Skill Equity Assessment

Job	Skill	Enjoyed using this skill (Rate on a scale of 1-10) 1=Didn't love 10 = Love	Is this skill in demand in the current marketplace	List three other industries or jobs you could use this skill in (if applicable)?
Paralegal	Legal Writing	10	YES	1. Online Content marketing (articles, blogs) 2. Copywriter (website content, autoresponders 3. Ghostwriter

Do you see how I took just one of my favorite skills, legal writing, and transferred it over to the current marketplace? I did use my writing skills after I left the legal field. I knew this was a valuable skill, and I created several ways to use it to get paid. Start thinking about some of your skills that you can use in new ways to get paid.

EXERCISE: Complete the chart for every job you've had. For any skills you rate seven or above, research how you can utilize those skills to get paid in the current marketplace. If you want to be location-independent, instead of location-stuck, look for opportunities online that don't require your physical presence. Many jobs are now virtual.

Social Equity

Next, list the people you have developed relationships with over the years. Networking is essential on your new career path.

Being in the publishing world, I have relationships with editors, ghostwriters, book publicists, media specialists, and others. You must invest the time to nurture your relationships.

I invest time in relationships with those in my network. This allows me to learn more about their businesses, and I am able to refer clients to professionals that I know can help solve their problems. I also receive referrals from others in my network.

Below is a chart you can use to list colleagues and customers you enjoyed interacting with at your previous job(s). Maintaining relationships will be vital as you create your new career path.

I wish I had done this after I left the legal field. I think many of the attorneys I worked with would be interested in writing a book or would have referred clients to me for my bestselling author program. I was short-sighted and didn't keep in touch with many of these people.

Social Equity Assessment

Colleagues and Customers you enjoy interacting with.	Do you have their contact information?	How can they help you find new opportunities?	Make a plan to stay in touch.

INFLUECE EQUITY

Influence equity describes the ability to have your ideas heard, the connections you've learned to use, and the resources that others make available to you to get your job done.

It's different than social equity in that these connections have resources that can help you get your ideas heard. They may have a large social media platform, a top-rated iTunes podcast, or they are a radio host or a YouTube influencer.

In the chart below, list the people with influence that you have met while working at your job(s) with whom you want to nurture and further develop a relationship.

Influence Equity Assessment

Names of people with Influence.	Do you have their contact information?	How can they help you find new opportunities?	Make a plan to stay in touch.

Financial Equity Assessment

List the income along with any perks you receive in return for your know-how and commitment for the job you do.

Job	Income	Can you get paid in another way that is location independent? Maybe with perks, or barter?	Is there a way to continue to get income in a different way?

The key is to take your equity that you've built up from all the jobs you've had and apply it in new ways in the modern marketplace.

Listed below are more than a dozen places you can immediately find work. Familiarize yourself with these websites as you move toward controlling your destiny instead of being solely dependent on a job:

- Upwork
- FlexJobs
- LinkedIn Jobs
- Fiverr
- Remote.co
- Simply Hired
- Smashing Magazine jobs
- Working Nomads
- Authentic jobs
- WP Hired
- Freelancer.com
- Problogger jobs
- Krop
- Etsy
- Guru
- Writers Work
- Task Rabbit
- Postmates

Digital Nomads

You may have heard the term "Digital Nomads." These are people who use technology to work, live, play, and travel when they want and where they want.

I consider myself a Digital Nomad because I can work from anywhere as long as I have an internet connection. I am free from commuting in rush hour traffic, tiny cubicles, strict schedules, and I work according to my own rules.

You can also start using the equity that you've built up in your jobs to become a Digital Nomad.

I promise that once you get a taste of freedom from the corporate world, you won't want to go back.

Just recently, one of my clients joined my Bestselling Author program begging me to help him get out of "job prison."

12 weeks and a lot of hard work later, he now has a #1 bestselling book, has been featured on platforms like Yahoo Finance, has sold over $20K of his online course on the back-end of his book, and has a new stream of income now. I'm happy to say that my client was able to quit his high-stress job and can work from home and be with his wife and two daughters.

When you set an intention and work hard, anything is possible!

Chapter 3: Re-Vision

Where there is no vision, the people perish.

It's time to create a new vision for your life and your career path.

You've probably lost sight of, or maybe you never had, a clear vision for your career path and have fallen into the consumerism and job trap.

The status quo has been to buy as many luxury items as possible to live like a King or Queen. If you can afford the monthly payments, you're okay.

That might have worked during a booming economy, but as COVID-19 is taking away people's livelihoods by the minute, this is no longer sustainable.

I just read today as I'm writing these words that more than 4 million people could not make their mortgage payments this month. In her book, "The Gig Economy," author Diane Mulcahy, said:

"Middle-class Americans are overinvested in housing, and that investment is not paying off."

Unfortunately, home ownership and a 30-year mortgage are causing many Americans to stay stuck because they are overextended. Additionally, the return on that investment from 1983 to 2013 was only 3.5 percent compared to stocks, which was about 9 percent during the same period, according to Diane Mulcahy.

If you had zero income for the next twelve months, what would that mean to you? Would you lose everything?

If your answer is YES, then it's time to reconsider EVERYTHING you've been doing.

A post on the *Credit Donkey* titled, "23 Scientific Reasons why Renting is Better," says this about homeownership:

"Homeownership has long been considered the culmination of a person's adult life, a moment when they've finally achieved the American Dream. However, more and more Americans are foregoing the 30-year mortgage and opting to rent instead."

Homeownership is not for everyone, especially in the COVID-19 ever-changing world in which we live. Even though it has been the status quo for a long time, this is one critical area to look at as you begin to re-Vision your life and determine what you want to create going forward.

I once owned a million-dollar house with a million-dollar mortgage, and guess what? I rent now. I have no unexpected expenses, my rent is affordable, and I have the freedom to relocate at any time. I've been renting for about four years, and I have a beautiful (somewhat expensive) house on the water. I would not want to spend close to a million dollars for this house, but I get to enjoy it for a fraction of the cost.

It's a personal choice, but the truth is, "The less you have to PAY, the more you can PLAY!"

Many of our choices were based on our early influences, such as our parents, our families, and society as a whole. If we don't take the time now to reflect on our personal version of success, we can easily continue living someone else's vision of success.

A good friend of mine, who recently got divorced, and has a mortgage on his $450K home, told me that he is considering selling his house (that the bank owns and he would end up paying over $800K over 30 years).

He wants to buy some land and live in an RV. He said he couldn't see himself staying in his corporate job for 30 years just to pay his mortgage.

I'm sure there's a reason the Tiny House movement is growing rapidly as many younger people aren't buying into the vision that our parents and grandparents had of the 30-year mortgage, staying in debt, and retiring when we are too old to enjoy it.

We must turn away from these external versions of success or what we think we are "supposed" to do and get clarity about our internal desires and dreams.

Do you want the outdated American dream of the expensive house, the car, the 2.5 kids, and retirement when you're too old to enjoy it? This is known as the ***deferred life plan,*** which Tim Ferris discusses in his bestselling book, "The 4-Hour Work Week."

It's time to stop postponing your life.

Mark Twain said it best, "Whenever you find yourself on the side of the majority, it is time to pause and reflect."

Is your vision of success a cubicle dweller, working hard in a 9-to-5 soul-sucking environment, in exchange for (some) relaxation on the weekends and the occasional keep-it-short-or-get-fired vacation?

I don't want a deferred life. I want to enjoy my life NOW, and one of the main ways to do that is by ***separating time from money.***

The traditional way we have lived for decades is to trade hours for dollars. Tim Ferris was right when he said:

> *"...the perfect job is one that takes the least time."*

You must make this paradigm shift and separate your time from money going forward.

Start thinking about value instead of hourly wages. I get paid to bring value to my clients, and I don't charge hourly rates. In fact, I haven't had hourly rates for more than a decade. When you don't trade your time for money, you can write your own paycheck because you are not limited by how many hours you can work.

It's how I've built a multi-six-figure business, and am working on creating my 7-figure business now!

Would you like to create cash flow on autopilot that is not connected to how many hours you work?

Awesome!

Right now, I want you to imagine me waving a beautiful magic wand in front of you. Voila! You have enough money in your bank account to pay your living expenses for the next two years.

I want you to tap into your imagination and create your perfect career path and dream life.

This is not about job searching; this is about soul searching.

The truth is most of us would rather be *job searching* than *soul searching*.

Why?

Because it's easier to skip soul searching and just find another job because then we don't have to ask ourselves the tough questions like…

- What brings me alive?
- What does my soul want to do?
- What brings me joy?
- What needs to die so my dreams can live?

It is easier to live a *default* life than an *intentional* life.

Let's Play the Nine Lives Game

We all have heard that cats have nine lives. Perhaps that is why cats are so laid back and calm. They know if they fall, they will land on their feet and can try again. For a moment, let's pretend that you have nine lives, too.

STEP 1: Select your nine lives.

If you had nine lives and could have nine different occupations—what would you be? (Examples: Writer, Gourmet Chef, Professor, Race Car Driver, Athlete, Writer, Chocolatier.) Don't use your logical mind; use your creative mind and give yourself permission to dream!

Barbara Sher, author of "I Could Do Anything if I Only Knew What It Was" (excellent book by the way; I highly recommend it) says that we've been trained to **believe that we only get one choice in our lives**. That isn't true at all. We have an endless number of options, so we really need to **learn how to manage these choices.**

Once you have determined your nine lives, answer the questions below, which will help you better manage your choices. We can't do everything at once, but if we manage our time better, we can do a lot more than we are doing right now.

STEP 2: Review your list, then answer these questions:

- Which of the nine lives above can you focus on this year?
- When that one is complete, which one can you focus on next year?
- Which of the nine lives can you focus on for 30 minutes to an hour each day?
- Which one can you do on occasion?

If you're feeling stuck or just don't know what new career path you want to create or investigate, I have a solution.

Pivot Planet to the Rescue

I have great news for you! Pivot Planet (**www.pivotplanet.com**) can arrange for you to test drive your dream job or dream business. After all, it would be a great misfortune to quit your job only to find out down the road that you really didn't like what you thought was going to be your *dream* job or *dream* business.

I love the concept of working with Pivot Planet, which provides virtual mentorship with real people in real careers. Here is an excerpt from their website:

- "Since 2004, Pivot Planet's founder, Brian Kurth, and his Vocation Vacations career mentorship team have provided thousands of one-to-three-day in-person mentorship experiences to people exploring a new career or a path not taken.
- For as little as $50 per hour, Pivot Planet connects people around the world looking to "pivot" from an existing career to a new career or enhance their current job skills with expert advisors working in hundreds of fields. These advisors offer affordable,

one-on-one video and phone sessions. Pivot Planet also offers the option of in-person mentorship with some of its advisors.

- Pivot Planet goes beyond connecting online, career coaching or corporate outplacement.
- Pivot Planet is the resource for finding real-life career and start-up business advice shared by experienced advisors who can answer your questions and offer insights into their profession. Anywhere. Anytime."

I love it!

I encourage you to test drive your dream job or business idea with **Pivot Planet** as part of your exploration. Here's an example of some of the hundreds of advisors they have:

- Travel Writer
- Chief Technology Officer
- Actor
- Dog Daycare Owner
- Digital Strategist
- Make-up Artist
- Magazine Editor
- Distiller
- Music Producer
- Filmmaker
- Fitness Trainer
- Nonprofit Director
- Home Stager

- Pet Resort Owner
- Pastry Chef
- Pastor
- Publisher
- Psychologist
- Professional Poker Player
- Private Investigator
- Wine Tasting Room Owner

And the list goes on and on!

Check it out yourself at **PivotPlanet.com/browse**. This is a great way to try out your ideas before taking the plunge!

Remember, you don't have to pick *one* thing. Select your top 10, then narrow it down to three. Switching careers can be so much more fun when you think of it as an experiment and are not afraid of just testing and trying things out!

I have another exercise for you…

I want you to write down what your perfect day would look like. Use your imagination and dream bigger than you ever have before.

You can begin your new career from *any* place in the world. Remember, you have enough money saved to pay two years of living expenses in your bank account. It's a good start, but it won't last forever, so you have to create a new way to earn a living based on the new career path habits you learned in Chapter 1.

Let's review those new Career Path Habits one more time.

1. Be a brand, not an employee.

2. Don't expect security from one job. Expect to hold multiple positions throughout your career and have a variety of diverse work experiences. Job security is a myth.

3. Diversifying creates security. Create income security by creating multiple streams of income.

4. Stop trading time for money and start creating value.

5. The Gig Economy is here to stay.

6. Stop looking for a job, and create a more aligned and satisfying career that helps you achieve your vision of professional and personal success.

7. Have an opportunity mindset (instead of an employee mindset) to learn on the job, at your own pace, and in lower-risk situations.

8. Think access, not ownership. Keep your fixed costs low so you can easily adjust to changes in your earnings.

9. Schedule time off and vacations frequently.

10. Always be learning. Learners are earners.

I recommend you listen to some relaxing music, light a candle, do a meditation, and then after you have quieted your mind, begin the exercise below.

Write the details in your journal!

Here are some details you might consider:

- Where are you living?
- What time of day or night do you work?
- Do you work from home?
- Do you travel?
- Who is around you?
- Who works for you?
- Are you a freelancer?
- How many freelance gigs do you have?
- Do you own your own business?
- Do you have a job that you love?
- How do you spend your day?
- What time do you wake up?
- How much money do you get paid?
- How do you get paid?
- Do you earn any passive income? If so, from where?
- Who are your dream clients?
- Do you own or rent a home?
- Are you a digital nomad?

Write out your perfect day below (or in a journal if you prefer)

Dreams do come true, but you have to give yourself permission to dream first! I think we're afraid to dream big because we fear our dreams won't come true, or we may even fear success. By allowing yourself to create and live your dream life, you will be an example to others and inspire them to change their lives and to have what they want.

I thank God for all the mentors, coaches, and teachers I've had along the way that broke through their old limiting beliefs in order to create their dream life. They have all encouraged me to do the same.

You can do it, and this is just the beginning.

Remember what my boss said to me when he hired me for that outside sales job, "We hired you because you don't have any bad habits."

To create your new career path and dream life, it's important to put the past and your old career path habits away and embrace the new ones.

I'm excited that you are working towards more freedom than you've ever had before.

Next, we're going to talk about renewing your priorities and values so you can experience authentic alignment on your new career path.

Chapter 4: Renew

It's time to renew your priorities, values, and commitment to yourself.

I once dated a man who was divorced with three grown children; two were in college, and one was in high school. He had previously been married for 17 years, and I "assumed" he was a family man.

As things progressed, I saw that he was married to his job as a police officer/detective and not his family. He worked two 40-hour per week jobs and had been doing so for more than twenty years. Things were completely out of balance in his life, and everything took a backseat to his jobs, including me.

Coming from a big and very close Italian family, one of my top priorities and values is "family time." Because we were not aligned in that area, it caused a lot of problems in our relationship. Eventually, we broke up.

The same holds true for your career path. If your top priorities and values revolve around family, yet your job consumes all of your time (And when you're not physically at work, you're still thinking about work or doing work), then you won't feel fulfilled and happy because you have abandoned that priority.

This chapter will help you clarify your priorities and values as you begin to create your new career path while renewing your commitment to yourself.

It's time to put your desires and dreams first. Many of us have sacrificed ourselves and our dreams for far too long. It's time to put yourself at the top of the list.

Circle 5-10 Core Values that are important to you; then narrow it down to your top 3.

- Truth
- Self-worth
- Safety
- Relationships
- Respect
- Freedom
- Honesty
- Integrity
- Dignity
- Kindness
- Service
- Inner peace
- Love
- Trust
- Equality
- Faith
- Justice
- Honor
- Charity
- Joy
- Wholeness
- Simplicity
- Hope
- Attitude

Which one would you be willing to die for?

Have you been living your life with these core values, or have you traded them in for other things?

No judgment. It's just important to see what we have been abandoning or neglecting.

Next, let's look at your priorities.

In Abraham Maslow's hierarchy of needs, he talks about how important it is to take care of our lower needs before we can achieve our full potential. Maslow developed the following hierarchy of needs:

- **Basic Needs** – Physiological Needs: Food, Water, Warmth, Rest
- **Safety Needs** – Security, Safety
- **Belongingness and Love Needs** – Intimate Relationships, Friends
- **Esteem Needs** – Prestige and Feelings of Accomplishment
- **Self-Actualization** – Achieving One's Full Potential, Including Creative Activities

Anyone struggling to get their basic physical and/or psychological needs met is not in a frame of mind to focus on self-actualization.

We all have basic priorities, such as food, shelter, warmth, love, attention, and safety. Once those needs are met, we can look at our other "higher level" needs, such as feelings of accomplishment, self-esteem, achieving our potential, and creativity.

Like many people, I've struggled with low self-esteem and had to do a lot of emotional work to overcome that. As a result of that work, I make better choices and have learned to use my intuition and to connect with my heart and my soul. I have learned to put myself, my values, and my priorities first. When there is an imbalance in my life or my relationships, this is where I first look.

Let's do a priority assessment.

Consider the following priorities:

- Job
- Health/Fitness
- Relationships/Love
- Family
- Self Esteem
- Creativity
- Financial Health/Security
- Fun/Relaxation/Downtime
- Spirituality/Religion

We don't have to choose "one" priority, as they are all important. If your career path has caused you to abandon, neglect, or ignore your priorities, then now is the time to look at that. You can't change what you don't see.

If *family* is a top priority for you, but you work 60-80 hours per week, then you are placing your job over your family. You may say that the reason you work so many hours is to provide for your family, but what good is that when you are not spending any time with your family, you are stressed out and preoccupied with your job?

It's time to be radically honest and create a brand new future.

There was a time when I worked three jobs to take care of my three young children. Even though my children were my top priority, I wasn't able to spend much time with them because I was always working. I felt guilty being away from them, and that guilt developed because I had abandoned my #1 priority — family.

Of course, working and taking care of our families is essential, but we also need to look clearly at how much of our time we give to our jobs and how little time we spend with our family.

I have redesigned my life now to work 4-5 hours per day, four days per week. I spend the rest of my time revolved around my other priorities, such as family, creativity, health, relationships, fun, and more!

So you don't have to pick one priority, but I encourage you to assess where you are with each of these universal priorities. On a scale of 1-10 (1 being low and 10 being high), write the number you feel you are at right now for each priority.

- Health/Fitness: _____
- Relationships/Love: _____
- Family: _____
- Self Esteem: _____
- Creativity: _____
- Financial Health/Security: _____
- Fun/Relaxation/Downtime: _____
- Spirituality/Religion: : _____

I included "downtime" in this list because I don't believe we have to fill up every minute with scheduled activities. We are addicted to being busy and feeling guilty when we are just chilling out or relaxing with no agenda.

Plato said, "You can discover more about a person in an hour of play than in a year of conversation."

Playing is light-hearted and not so serious. We played as children, and we work hard as adults.

I became so depleted after 17 years in the legal field because I was working all the time and had no "play" time.

George Bernard Shaw said, "We don't stop playing because we grow old; we grow old because we stop playing."

Right now, my two-year-old granddaughter lives with me, and the only thing she wants to do is play! It's awesome because it allows me to play and have fun without a plan. We have *play deficits* as adults, and we need to carve out that downtime for playing and just being silly and having fun.

Now that you have assessed each of these areas, make one simple change in each of your low-ranked areas. Here are some examples:

- **Health/Fitness**: Go for a walk after dinner with the kids
- **Relationships/Love**: Go on a date night once per week with your partner.
- **Family**: Stop working overtime and commit to having dinner at least three nights per week together.
- **Self Esteem**: Read a self-help book or go to therapy.
- **Creativity**: Find a hobby that is fun and enjoyable.
- **Financial Health/Security**: Assess your current finances on paper.
- **Fun/Relaxation/Downtime**: End your workday at 5 pm.
- **Spirituality/Religion**: Meditate daily.

You don't have to change everything at once. In fact, it's best if you make one or two small changes at a time.

Some books on habits that I love are "Elastic Habits" by Stephen Guide and "Atomic Habits" by James Clear.

I love this quote from "Atomic Habits:"

"All big things come from small beginnings. The seed of every habit is a single, tiny decision. But as that decision is repeated, a habit sprouts and grows stronger. Roots entrench themselves and branches grow. The task of breaking a bad habit is like uprooting a powerful oak within us. And the task of building a good habit is like cultivating a delicate flower one day at a time."

He says not to focus on goals, but to focus on actions and systems instead.

Tiny habits are little habits that are part of a larger system and the building blocks of remarkable results.

So don't underestimate starting with these tiny changes. They are both small and mighty at the same time.

As we repeat them over time, they become stronger.

Another big takeaway from James Clear's book is "True behavior is identity change."

- The goal is not to read a book; the goal is to become a reader.
- The goal is not to run a marathon but to become a runner.
- The goal is not to learn an instrument but to become a musician.

Who do you want to become?

When you align your behavior with your identity, you start acting like the type of person you believe yourself to be.

I am a reader. I probably read 50-100 books per year. It is part of my identity. I am also a yoga enthusiast. Yoga has helped me relax, reduce stress, and also be more flexible and limber.

As you begin looking at your core values and priorities, start thinking about your identity and who you want to become.

- **Do you want to be a family man or family woman?**
- **Do you want to be a cyclist?**
- **Do you want to be a vegetarian?**
- **Do you want to be a writer?**

Our identity emerges out of our habits. Frequent action of tiny habits will yield remarkable results.

James Clear says, "If you can get 1 percent better each day for one year, you'll end up thirty seven-times better by the time you're done. Conversely, if you get 1 percent worse each day for one year, you'll decline to nearly zero."

Our habits are the compound interest of self-improvement.

If you want to change your career path and your life, you need to make small changes that you will repeat over time.

To renew our lives, the old has to die for the new to live.

Let's renew your commitment to yourself and to your values and priorities:

I renew my commitment to myself and my dreams.

I renew my commitment to my top three values which are:

1. *
2. *
3. *

I renew my commitment to aligning my life with my priorities:

- Health/Fitness
- Relationships/Love
- Family
- Self Esteem
- Creativity
- Fun/Relaxation/Downtime
- Spirituality/Religion

I believe you should do this assessment every 3-12 months. If you only do it one time, the chances are high that you'll forget about it and go back to your old ways.

Write down these priorities and values on index cards and make reading them part of your morning and/or evening rituals.

You are in the process of a transformation – much like the caterpillar to a butterfly. Honor your passion for emerging into something new.

Chapter 5: Reposition

Reposition yourself from an employee to a brand.

When I worked for the 600+ person law firm in Washington, D.C., I felt like an invisible cog of their well-oiled corporate machine whose primary focus was billable hours. I was an employee, and they could have referred to me as a number (instead of using my name) because while working there, I felt like a faceless number.

For years, they told me when to show up, what to do, when to do it, how to do it and added more work for not enough pay.

No wonder I was miserable at the end of those 17 years.

As I moved into the world of entrepreneurship, I transitioned from being told what to do to deciding what I wanted to do.

I've gone from employee to entrepreneur/brand, and the difference is huge. I only answer to my clients who hire me because of the brand I have created around myself.

So, what is a brand?

Jeff Bezos, the founder of Amazon, once said, "Your personal brand is what people say about you when you leave the room."

Characteristics of BRAND YOU

- The added value you bring to others
- Your competitive advantage
- Your reputation
- The target market you are attracting

- Your relevancy in the marketplace
- Your specialization

Being a "brand" doesn't require you to start your own business; instead, think of yourself as a brand, even if you work for someone else or as a subcontractor.

Let's take a look at each of these areas.

The Added Value You Bring to Others

Remember, we don't trade hours for dollars; we bring value to others. It's time to start thinking of ourselves as valuable people who enrich and enhance the lives of the people we work with.

My son works for Lexus and makes six figures selling cars. In fact, he is one of the top salespeople at Lexus. Imagine if he was working for an hourly wage. Even at a high hourly rate of $40 per hour, working 40 hours per week, he would not be making anywhere close to what he makes now.

When you know your value, you don't settle for crumbs.

Over the years, I've been fortunate to work with two very talented high-ticket business coaches who both advised me to increase my fees. I was an "underearner" — someone who has the potential to earn more money, but stays in lower-paying jobs or undercharges.

I had an "hourly rate" mentality, and until I shifted it to the *value* I was bringing to my clients, I was missing out. Since then, I've embraced my value and consequently have tripled my rates over the years.

One benefit of charging high-ticket prices is the quality of people you work with (action takers, decision makers, professionals) is stellar. I've sold low-ticket, and I've sold high-ticket, and I will choose high-ticket every time.

When someone is paying you high-ticket rates, they show up in a much bigger and more committed way. Because I am charging high-ticket, I'm able to devote my time and energy to a small number of clients, rather than chasing hundreds or thousands of clients.

I know many people who sell $97-$997 online courses or programs, and that's fine if it's something you do in addition to your high-ticket, high-value offer.

Doing outside sales for ten years, I learned to sell packages that included the results my clients desired. People don't want information as much as they want transformation. I can only deliver change to people by selling high-ticket because then I can focus and devote my energy and time to those select clients. If my entire business revolved around a $97 online course, I would burn out trying to get clients into that course continually, and my clients would not get my dedicated time and energy.

I was fortunate enough to sell a high-ticket item when I was in outside sales. When I started my online business and sold low-ticket, I quickly realized that it takes the same amount of energy to sell low-ticket as it does to sell high-ticket.

So, focus on high-ticket and providing the best experience and getting results for others. When people feel valued, they will rave about you.

I have received so many wonderful testimonials from my clients because I am committed to their success and to the value I bring to them.

Do you value your gifts, skills, experiences, and talents? Are you ready to start charging more for your unique gifts, skills, expertise, and talents?

When you are clear what your competitive advantage is, I promise you will have no problem charging what you're worth!

Your Competitive Advantage

Your competitive advantage makes you unique. It's your personal story, what you have overcome, and your talents, gifts, skills, and wisdom.

There is no one like you.

In book publishing, I think one of my competitive advantages is that I am 100% in love with books and authors! Also, I am a book-a-holic, as I live, eat, and breathe books. Since 2019, I've been writing a book a month. So I'm not only working to help authors succeed; I am an author, and that gives me a competitive advantage.

List Some of Your Competitive Advantages

_____

_____

_____

_____

_____

_____

_____

_____

My Competitive Advantages

- 17 years in legal working in litigation, which gives me a unique skillset in the publishing world
- 10 years of outside sales experience
- Three years as a newspaper reporter
- Raised three children on my own (independent, multi-tasker)
- High-level tech skills
- Writing skills
- High passion for books
- Published author
- Have written over a dozen books
- Not afraid to sell high-ticket products and services
- Love teaching others
- Believe that my client's success is my success
- Committed to authors

I refer some of my clients to a brilliant ghostwriter, who is a full-time attorney, a Judge, and a published author of five books. She has a unique skillset, as you can see. Because of her background and competitive advantage, she can charge high ticket.

Don't underestimate or take for granted your competitive advantage.

Once you know your competitive advantage, it's time to look at your reputation.

Your Reputation

We live and work in a transparent world, and your reputation can quickly be ruined online. I have worked very hard over the years to keep my reputation spotless and clear. Of course, there have been some misunderstandings with a few clients, but I have always bent over backwards to make my clients happy and ensure they are satisfied with the results. I believe reputation is everything in business.

As you begin designing a new career path, you must prioritize your reputation, especially if you are going to start your own business or work as a subcontractor.

When my son sells a car at Lexus, he always asks the buyer to write a review. Reviews are everything in his business. Strive for excellence and admit if you make a mistake and correct it as fast as you can.

Which Target Market Are You Attracting?

I recently wrote the script for a new webinar, part of which identifies the internal and external objections my potential clients might have. When I shared one of the "internal objections" with my business coach, she recommended that I didn't use that particular objection in the webinar and said, "Michelle, think about WHO you will be attracting if you say that."

She was right. I would have been attracting the "newbie" crowd who didn't have any business experience—the opposite of what I wanted. My goal was to attract high-level, already successful entrepreneurs and business owners who wanted to write a book to advance their business.

Your brand and the words you use are what attracts people to you. So, think about who you want to work with and who you want to attract.

One of my favorite books on business and marketing is: "Bee-ing Attraction: What Love Has To Do With Business and Marketing." Authors Jan Stringer and Alan Hickman have a unique perspective about this topic:

> *"You will learn to become more creative and imaginative as you design a plan for what you want others to expect of you rather than attempting to live life by what you think others might want from you."*

The Bee-ing Attraction method has four parts:

1. Describe the qualities and attributes that are a perfect fit for you.
   Example:
   - My clients value our time.
   - My clients value their time.
   - My clients pay on time.
   - My clients pay our full fee.
   - M clients keep their appointments.
   - My clients are intelligent and have good common sense.
   - My clients are peaceful, calm, and kind.
   - My clients are decisive.

2. What makes my perfect customer and me tick?
   Example:
   - Helping others find their voice.
   - Shining the light for others to reach their full potential.
   - Connecting with people through laughter.

- Working with others to build a legacy with their business.

3. Specify what you want your perfect customer to expect of you. Example:
    - My perfect customers expect me to earn six figures.
    - My perfect customers expect me to act professionally.
    - My perfect customers expect me to have a team to support their goals.
    - My perfect customers expect me to be a published author.
    - My perfect customers expect me to have a client training portal.
    - My perfect customers expect me to respond to them in 24 hours.

4. Declare who you get to BEE to attract what you want and give the Bee-ing a title. Example:
    - I am Bee-ing a million-dollar business owner
    - I am Bee-ing the top real estate producer in my state.
    - I am Bee-ing a 6-Figure Author.
    - I am Bee-ing a motivational speaker.

I highly recommend you read this book and go through all of these exercises. Define who you want to be and what makes you tick.

It's essential to connect with what makes you tick while sharing your unique talents and gifts.

It's important to love what you do.

When a business owner (or employee or subcontractor) loves what they are doing, you know and feel it. You receive the warmth of their enthusiasm and the energy of their excitement. Many times, we follow our logical minds when it comes to our career path, rather than our hearts.

I stayed stuck in a career for which I no longer had a passion, and believe me, everyone around me knew it, including my bosses and co-workers. I was mentally checked out because I did not want to be there.

It's important to create a heart-centered career path because people will be attracted to that energy more than anything else.

Answer the following questions:

- What gets you up in the morning?
- What keeps you burning the midnight oil?
- What is your soul purpose?
- Why are you here?

Which of these "tick" words give you energy?

- Freedom
- Creativity
- Beauty
- Love
- Teaching
- Magic
- Justice
- Transformation
- Equality
- The Environment

For me, Freedom, Creativity, and Transformation give me energy.

What are your three tick words?

1. _____
2. _____
3. _____

As you get clearer in these areas, you'll see how you start to attract those people into your life. Light attracts light.

As we reposition ourselves, it's time to think about our relevancy in the marketplace.

Your Relevancy

Relevancy is important because the marketplace is continually changing. Consider companies that are now out of business that previously dominated their spaces:

- Blockbuster
- Sears
- Borders Bookstore

These companies did not pivot fast enough in the evolving world. They rested on their laurels and what got them to become successful, didn't guarantee that they would stay there.

Blockbuster could no longer compete with streaming services. Sears could no longer compete with Amazon and Walmart. Borders Bookstore did not embrace digital book technology fast enough and was forced to close its brick-and-mortar locations.

Stay relevant. Stay up to date and know that nothing stays the same. Things are either contracting or expanding.

In 2015, I created my first client training portal to support my high-ticket program. In 2020, I recorded all new videos because the technology, processes, systems, and resources have changed so much over the past five years and the old videos were outdated.

I needed to make sure my content and training materials are relevant to my clients.

When I started working in law firms in 1983, I learned to type on an electric typewriter, and then we upgraded to the IBM memory select typewriter. When WordPerfect, the first word processing system was introduced, I became an expert at using it until Microsoft Word took over. The changes in technology and processes were never-ending.

I did not want to learn Word because I loved WordPerfect, but that's what everyone was using, and we had to stay relevant.

Is there an area in your life or business where you are clinging to the past?

Stay relevant, and you'll never be broke.

Your Specialization

"It is those who concentrate on but one thing at a time who advance this world."

– Og Mandino

In his book, "The One Thing," author Gary Keller, founder of Keller Real Estate, says:

"Teaching is my ONE Thing and has been for almost 30 years. At first, it was teaching clients about the market and how to make great decisions. Next, it was teaching salespeople in the classroom, during sales meetings, and one-on-one. Later it was teaching business classes. Then it became teaching high performers, models, and strategies for high achievement, and the last ten years, it has been teaching seminars on specific life-building principles. What I teach is what I then coach and is supported by what I write."

When I read that in his book, it was eye-opening to me as I always thought my "one thing" was writing. But just like Gary, my one thing is teaching. I love to teach, and I do that in many ways, and one of those ways is writing.

Here is some great advice from Gary Keller:

> "Pick a direction, start marching down that path, and see how you like it. Time brings clarity and if you find you don't like it, you can always change your mind. It's your life."

My only caveat to that advice is know when to quit.

While I have a lot of favorite authors, Seth Godin is one of my top three authors. His books are transformational and force me to think outside the box.

In his book, "The Dip: A Little Book That Teaches You When to Quit (And When to Stick)," Godin says this about quitting:

> *"Most people quit. They just don't quit successfully… Strategic quitting is the secret to successful organizations. Reactive quitting and serial quitting are the bane of those that strive (and fail) to get what they want. And most people do just that. They quit when it's painful and stick when they can't be bothered to quit."*

Sounds weird, right – strategic quitting?

Yes, you need to know when to quit and when to stick.

So, how do you know?

First, you must understand what the "dip" is that Seth talks about in the book. The dip is basically the long slog between beginning something new and mastery.

He said, "If you can't make it through the dip, then don't start."

He explains that people who make millions of dollars have entered fields with steep dips and they have succeeded through the dip.

The key is to know before you start something whether you have the resources and will to get to the end.

Seth goes on to say:

> *"Average is for Losers. Quitting at the right time is difficult. Most of us don't have the guts to quit. Worse, when faced with the Dip, sometimes we don't quit. Instead, we get mediocre. The most common response to the dip is to play it safe."*

If you want to be a superstar, you must do something exceptional. Average is for losers. Quit or be exceptional.

I've quit a lot of jobs and a lot of businesses in my life, some not soon enough. I've invested too much time and energy, knowing I wasn't going to be successful.

It's great to try new things, but we must be honest with ourselves and then use strategic quitting.

If there is a long "dip," then the payoff is probably very high, which means it's designed to weed out average people.

Don't quit just because things get hard. If you know you have the resources and can get to the end, then stick with it.

Figuring out your specialization takes time.

This work is revealed over time and not in one big aha moment.

It is not a linear path; we stumble into clarity. Exploration is the key. Don't be afraid to not know the answers. Dabble on the wild side and your child side.

Maybe right now, your specialization is that you know the career path you are on is a dead-end, and a new career path is revealing itself day-by-day.

Try new things. Experiment. Know when to quit and when not to.

Follow your desires and take the next visible step in front of you.

Don't just sit around daydreaming. Take action and get in the arena.

I'll end this chapter with one of my favorite quotes by Theodore Roosevelt:

> *"It is not the critic who counts; not the man who points out how the strong man stumbles, or where the doer of deeds could have done them better. The credit belongs to the man who is actually in the arena, whose face is marred by dust and sweat and blood; who strives valiantly; who errs, who comes short again and again, because there is no effort without error and shortcoming; but who does actually strive to do the deeds; who knows great enthusiasms, the great devotions; who spends himself in a worthy cause; who at the best knows in the end the triumph of high achievement, and who at the worst, if he fails, at least fails while daring greatly, so that his place shall never be with those cold and timid souls who neither know victory nor defeat."*

Are you in the arena with me?

Next, we are going to talk about repackaging your skills for the highest value in the marketplace.

Chapter 6: Repackage

Repackage your skills and the value you bring to the world.

In a blog post by author, speaker, and teacher, Seth Godin, he wrote:

> "Skill vs. Talent
>
> You're born with talent.
>
> You earn a skill.
>
> I don't think there are many situations where talent is the key driver of success. The biggest exception might be that a drive to acquire skill could be a talent…
>
> Assuming you have even once done the hard work to learn something important, then you have what you need to develop even more skills.
>
> Go do that.
>
> We need generosity and passion. And even more so, we need people who care to develop the skills to deliver on their promises."

Some people have natural-born talents that they cash in on, and others learn skills that they cash in on. And some do both.

You can use your existing skillset and natural talents and add new skills to create a new career path.

I was born with a natural talent for writing, but I had to learn different aspects of writing, such as copywriting, newspaper reporting, editing, formatting, publishing, and more.

To cash in on your expertise, answer these questions:

- What do people tell me I do well? Is there a high demand for this in the marketplace?

- What obstacles and problems have I overcome in my life? Could I help others do the same? Is there a high demand for this in the marketplace?

- What am I an expert at already? Is there a high demand for this in the marketplace?

- What skills can I learn that interest me and are in high demand in the marketplace?

Skill-Stacking is the Next Best Thing

After I left the corporate world, I very quickly realized that to be marketable and sought after, I needed to learn new skills that were in high demand.

So I added several new skills over time.

I call this SKILL-STACKING, and it's the best way to increase your value in the marketplace.

The first skill I decided to focus on when I started my online business was copywriting.

I was fortunate to connect with a local copywriter in my area, Yanik Silver. I was his student for many years; he taught me the art of copywriting. I knew that one skill would separate me from the competition, so I mastered that skill.

Joe Vitale, in his book, "Hypnotic Writing: How to Seduce and Persuade Customers with Only Your Words," says,

"There are three keys to the success of any direct marketing campaign, whether it's done online or off:

- *The list*
- *The offer*
- *The copy*"

Robert Collier, one of the most well-known copywriters in the world, said, "Your problem, then, is to find a point of contact with his (the reader's) interests, his desires, some feature that will flag his attention and make your letter stand out from all the others the moment he reads the first line."

Because I worked in litigation as a paralegal for many years, I knew the power of persuasion to win legal cases. It made sense to me that you could have a beautiful website, but if you had sub-standard copywriting, you would probably be broke because you wouldn't be able to convert visitors into customers.

Mastering copywriting paid off for me because it gave me the ability to write sales letters, emails, paid ads, and blog posts to sell courses and programs. Others who did not have this skill paid me for copywriting services, and at the time, I charged $997 for a long copy sales letter.

I'm sharing this with you because the more skills you can learn and become proficient at, the more options and value you will have in the new world.

The second skill I learned was sales, and that has paid off 10x! If you have a business and can't sell, then you'll be a broke business owner. Either learn how to sell or hire someone who is a master at it.

In addition to copywriting and sales, I developed the following skills over the years that have paid me dividends to this day:

- Website Design
- Search Engine Optimization (SEO)
- Publishing
- Cover Design
- Book Launches
- Writing books
- Sales Calls

I'm also an expert (self-taught) at a variety of software programs such as AWeber, Hootsuite, Leadpages, Amazon KDP, and others.

- What skills do you have that others would pay you to do?
- What skills would you like to learn and then get paid for using?

When I see people who are unemployed or stuck in a low-paying jobs, I know they haven't taken the time to develop new skillsets.

Skills Pay the Bills

The more skills you have, the more money you can make.

I first made money online by writing and selling online courses. Then, I added coaching to provide more personalized services. I also did website design, SEO, copywriting, and, eventually, publishing and launching books for myself and others. As a result, I now have multiple streams of six-figure income.

I attribute all of this to taking that first step in learning new skills and then stacking them to create value in the marketplace.

I've discovered that sometimes you spend a lot of time learning a new software program and then the market shifts and you have to decide whether to stay where you are or shift with the market. If you want to be successful, you must learn to shift quickly.

If you don't change, you'll stay broke.

Here's a story about two people in the same industry, detrimentally affected by the changes in their respective businesses because of COVID-19; one shifted quickly, and the other did not:

Gary was my personal trainer about six or seven years ago. Shortly after COVID-19 caused many businesses, including gyms, to close, he reached out to me asking if I wanted to do "virtual personal training." I accepted the invitation, paid him for five weeks of personal training, and am still working out with him.

As we were chatting, I asked him what ratio of in-person clients vs. virtual training clients he had. He told me prior to COVID-19, he was doing 80% in-person training and 20% virtual training. I was surprised to learn that he had started virtual training 11 years ago when one of his clients moved from Maryland to Hawaii but wanted to continue working out with him. The technology we have now did not exist 11 years ago, but he found a way to do it. He then offered that option to other clients..

When COVID-19 hit, he quickly pivoted and moved the 80% of his clients who were training in-person and transferred them to his virtual training sessions. Then he added new clients like me! He is still earning six figures and has not been financially impacted by the lockdown.

Not everyone in the same industry has been able to maintain their business. A colleague of mine told me about a personal trainer who couldn't pay his bills and support his family because the gym where he trained his clients was closed. He had applied for unemployment benefits but was denied. Then he applied for other government programs and did not qualify. He is struggling right now because he is either unwilling or unsure how to pivot.

Right now, it's pivot or get crushed.

There is a lot of chaos in the world, and somehow we need to make order out of it.

In his book, "Linchpin: Are you Indispensable" by Seth Godin, he says a linchpin is, "An individual who can walk into chaos and create order, someone who can invent, connect, create and make things happen."

Being a valuable creator is about connecting, creating, and reinventing yourself over and over and over. I don't see it as a negative. I love it! I became bored with most of the jobs I had after the first month because they were monotonous and there was very little change. Toys R Us, Sears, Kmart, Borders Bookstore, and others closed because they didn't want to change.

Are you ready to change and pivot?

We can start by changing the question we ask from "How do I get a job doing that?" to "How can I create a job doing that?"

When people ask me what I do, I usually answer, "I'm in publishing" because when I try to explain my entire business model, they look at me like I'm crazy.

I created a business that involves books because I love books, creating content, teaching, and helping authors succeed. I get paid to do what I love, and that happened because I created it.

If I went to any employment website, I'm positive I could never find a "job" doing what I do, making multiple six figures. It just doesn't exist.

Instead of looking for a job, create the perfect job using skills you already have (or quickly learn new ones) that are in high demand.

Recently, my former business coach sent an email to his list stating his business was growing exponentially, and he needed a sales enrollment coach to sell his program.

He spends about $1 million per year on Facebook ads and has a highly targeted and successful coaching business. It's so successful that he can't handle all the strategy session applications he receives.

If you had sales skills, you could work for him virtually and earn $1000 in commissions per sales call! Eight sales per month, and you are a 6-figure income earner.

List ten things you are an expert at (your skills) that you think you could charge others to do for them:

1. _____
2. _____
3. _____
4. _____
5. _____
6. _____
7. _____
8. _____
9. _____
10. _____

In my bestselling author program and business, I use all of the skills listed below (or pay others who have these skills) to make multiple six figures:

- Sales
- Copywriting/Writing
- Editing
- Formatting
- Cover Design
- Project Management
- Categories and Keywords Research
- Book Launches
- Networking
- Speaking

I developed this skill set over time; it didn't happen overnight.

The more skills you can combine, the more money you will make!

The purpose of this chapter is to look at your existing skillset and see the value it has in the current marketplace. How can you combine your current skillset and package it up to add value?

Also, you need to be continually learning new skills that are in high demand in the marketplace.

You don't need a new college degree, or year-long certification program to do this. Most of the skills I learned were from moderately priced online programs or from "on the job" experience.

Take, for example, web design. I did not go to school to learn how to design websites, and I'm not a programmer or coder. When I searched for ways to make money with my copywriting skills, I discovered that business owners desperately needed someone to write copy for their sites. Unfortunately, business owners don't seek out copywriters; what they do look for is website design.

I knew that in order to do what I really wanted to do – copywriting – I had to learn website design and then offer those skills to others.

I completed a 6-week online course on WordPress website design and became proficient at building websites quickly. I took my knowledge from outside sales and created packages, including "copywriting." Many prospects purchased this package because they unexpectedly realized they did not know how to write the content for their website.

After 30 days, I was making $4K to $10K per month doing "web design," which allowed me to use my copywriting skills to help others in the marketplace.

I did website design for almost five years, and it was very lucrative. You can make a lot of money in a short period of time when you have the skills that people want and are willing to pay others for.

There are generally two types of people:

1. People who are short on cash, but have a surplus of time.

2. People who are short on time, but have a surplus of cash.

If you find the people in group two, you can offer your services to them which will save them time and bring value to you both.

When learning new skills, I want to encourage you not to commit to long-term training programs; 90 days should be the maximum amount of time you allot for one training course.

One of my favorite authors (other than Seth Godin) is Mike Michalowicz, author of books like *Profit First, Clockwork, Pumpkin Plan,* and *Fix This Next.*

Mike is a brilliant business author and entrepreneur! I especially love that his business model involves building the profits into his books (which is what I teach my students to do in my Bestselling Author program).

In every book he writes, he offers a "certification" program at the end.

For example: At the end of his "Profit First" book, he asks if you want to become a Profit First Professional? Mike has a certification program designed for accountants, business coaches, financial planners, etc., and guess what? He can refer business to you because you are one of his certified experts?

That is certainly a quick way to start making money.

He offers certifications for all of his books, and here are a few examples below:

- Fix This Next (has a waitlist as of the time of this writing)
- Profit First
- Pumpkin Plan

Think about what skills interest you that you can learn and monetize. The following resources can help you get started:

- www.lynda.com (which is now "LinkedIn Learning") is a great place to learn skills with a low time and monetary investment ($19.99/month or $29.99/month). They have over 760 courses you can sign up for. Here's one I found that looks amazing:

https://www.lynda.com/Business-tutorials/Freelancing-Foundations/2825035-2.html

- https://www.masterclass.com/all-access-pass - the cost for masterclass is only $15 a month and there are some high-level teachers and courses on this platform.
- https://www.udemy.com/ - The courses are priced individually, but they are not expensive. And I like that they have a rating system.

If you have more money to invest, consider hiring a private business coach. That can accelerate your ability to start making money.

List ten skills that you have, or are interested in learning, and that are in high demand in our current marketplace.

1. _____
2. _____
3. _____
4. _____
5. _____
6. _____
7. _____
8. _____
9. _____
10. _____

To see if a skill is in high demand, check the websites listed above or online job boards like:

- Ziprecruiter
- Indeed
- LinkedIn
- Glassdoor
- Upwork
- CareerBuilder

If you see a lot of postings for jobs with these skillsets, then you know they are in high demand.

The skillsets listed below are very valuable right now in the online world:

- Copywriting
- Content Management
- Blog Writing
- Virtual Assistant
- Facebook Ads Manager
- Paid Ads Manager
- Sales Enrollment Specialist

There are many "Solo-preurs" like me that need support and are always looking for great talent.

Use your skills to pay the bills and repackage yourself as an expert that helps others get results!

Chapter 7: Re-Purpose

Discovering your purpose

Many times people get stuck in jobs and feel like they have no purpose. Then life becomes monotonous and meaningless.

There are many books written on the topic of finding your purpose, but as it relates to our careers, I believe that the following blog post written by author Elizabeth Gilbert will help you clarify what your purpose is and what it is not.

Elizabeth Gilbert's blog post:

"Dear Ones - I get a lot of questions from people who are seeking purpose and meaning in their lives. And I get a lot of questions from people who are seeking career advice — especially about creative careers. And I get a lot of questions from people who are absolutely confused about where their energy is going in life, and why.

For anyone out there who is seeking purpose and meaning and direction in their lives, I thought it might be useful today to define and differentiate four very important words that relate to HOW WE SPEND OUR TIME IN LIFE.

Are you ready?

The four very important words are:

HOBBY, JOB, CAREER, VOCATION/CALLING

These four words are often interconnected, but they are NOT interchangeable.

Too much of the time, we treat these words like they are synonyms, but they are NOT. They are gloriously distinct and should remain gloriously distinct. Each is wonderful and important in its own way. I think a lot of the pain and confusion that people face when they are trying to chart their lives is that they don't understand the meaning of these words — or the expectations and demands of each word.

So, let me break down what I consider to be the definitions and differences.

1. **HOBBY** — A hobby is something that you do for pleasure, relaxation, distraction, or mild curiosity. A hobby is something that you do in your spare time. Hobbies can come and go in life — you might try out a hobby for a while, and then move on to something new. I grew up in a family where everyone had hobbies (my grandmother made rag rugs; my grandfather made jewelry out of old spoons; etc.) and I have hobbies myself. Gardening was my hobby a few years ago; now it's Karaoke and collage-making. You can tell when something is a hobby because your attitude toward it tends to be relaxed and playful. The stakes are SUPER low with hobbies. Sometimes you might make a bit of money out of your hobby, but that's not the point — nor does it need to be. Hobbies are important because they remind us that not everything in life has to be about productivity and efficiency and profit and destiny. Hobbies are mellow. This is a wonderful reminder, and the concept should relax you. Hobbies prove that we have spare time — that we are not just slaves to the capitalist machine or to our own ambitions. You don't NEED a hobby, mind you, but it's awfully nice to have one. Even the word itself is adorable and non-threatening: HOBBY! What a cute word. Go get one. You have nothing to lose, and it'll probably make you happier. Also, my grandparents would

approve. Back before TV, everyone had hobbies. It's nice. No big deal.

2. **JOB** — You may not need a hobby, but you do absolutely need a job. Unless you have a trust fund, or just won the lottery, or somebody is completely supporting you financially... you need a job. Actually, I would argue that even if you DO have a trust fund or a winning lottery ticket or a generous patron, you should still have a job. I believe there is great dignity and honor to be found in having a job. A job is how you look after yourself in the world. I always had a job, or several jobs, back when I was an unpublished, aspiring writer. Even after I'd already published three books, I still kept a regular job, because I never wanted to burden my creativity with the responsibility of paying for my life. Artists often resent having jobs, but I never resented it. Having a job always made me feel powerful and secure and free. It was good to know that I could support myself in the world, and that I would never starve, no matter what happened with my creativity. Now, here's the most essential thing to understand about a job: IT DOESN'T HAVE TO BE AWESOME. Your job can be boring, it can be a drag, it can even be "beneath you". Jobs don't need to be soul-fulfilling. Really, they don't. I've had all kinds of weird and lame jobs; it doesn't matter, you don't need to love your job; you just need to have a job and do it with respect. Of course, if you absolutely hate your job, by all means look for another one, but try to be philosophical about why you have this job right now. (Some good philosophical reasons for staying in a crappy job right now include: You are taking care of yourself; you are supporting your beloved family; you are saving up for something important; you are paying off debts. The list of reasons to have a job — even a bad job — goes on and on, and honor abides within all those reasons.) Don't judge yourself about your job and never be a snob about anyone else's job. We live in a

material world and everyone has to do something for money, so just do whatever you have to do, collect your paycheck, and then go live the rest of your life however you want. Your job does not need to be how you define yourself; you can create your own definitions of your purpose and your meaning, pulled from deep within your imagination. A job is vital, but don't make it YOUR LIFE. It's not that big a deal. It's just a job — a very important and also not-at-all important thing.

3. **CAREER** — A career is different from a job. A job is just a task that you do for money, but a career is something that you build over the years with energy, passion, and commitment. You don't need to love your job, but I hope to heaven that you love your career — or else you're in the wrong career, and it would be better for you to quit that career and just go find yourself a job, or a different career. Careers are best done with excitement. Careers are huge investments. Careers require ambition, strategy, and hustle. Your career is a relationship with the world. I used to have jobs, but now I have a career. My career is: AUTHOR. That means: Professional Writer. When I think about my work in terms of my career, I need to make sure that I'm building good relationships in the publishing world, and making smart decisions, and managing myself well within a realm that is more public than private. I need to pay attention to what critics are saying about my work, and how my books are selling, and how well I'm meeting my deadlines. I need to tend to my career with respect and regard, or else I will lose it. I need to honor my contracts and my contacts. When I make decisions about my life, I need to think about whether this would be good or bad for my career. If I win an award, that's good for my career. If I get caught in a hotel room with a pile of cocaine and six exotic dancers, that's bad for my career. (Actually, now that I think about it, maybe that would be AWESOME for my career!

Gotta look into that! HA!) Let me make something very clear about careers: A career is a good thing to have if you really want one, but YOU DO NOT NEED TO HAVE A CAREER. There is absolutely nothing wrong with going through your entire life having jobs, and enjoying your hobbies, and pursuing your vocation, but never having "a career". A career is not for everyone. A career is a choice. But if you do make that choice, make sure that you really care about your career. Otherwise, it's just an exhausting marathon, for no reason. I really care about my career, but it's not the most important thing in my life. Not even close. The most important thing in my life is my....

4. **VOCATION** — The word "vocation" comes to us from the Latin verb "vocare" — meaning "to call". YOUR VOCATION IS YOUR CALLING. Your vocation is a summons that comes directly from the universe and is communicated through the YEARNINGS OF YOUR SOUL. While your career is about a relationship between you and the world; your vocation is about the relationship between you and God. Vocation is a private vow. Your career is dependent upon other people, but your vocation belongs only to you. You can get fired from your career, but you can never get fired from your vocation. Writing was my vocation long before I was lucky enough to get the career of an "Author" — and writing will always be my vocation, whether my career as an Author keeps working out or not. This is why I can approach my career with a certain sense of calm — because I know that, while I obviously care about career, I am not defined by it. When I consider my writing in terms of my career, I have to care what the world thinks about me. But when I consider my writing in terms of my vocation, I TRULY DO NOT GIVE A FUCK WHAT THE WORLD THINKS ABOUT ME. My career is dependent upon others; my vocation is entirely my own. The entire publishing world could vanish, and books could become

obsolete, and I would still be a writer — because that's my vocation. That's my deal with God. You do not need to make money from your vocation in order for it to have meaning. Writing had meaning for me LONG before you ever heard of me, and long before anyone else wanted me to do it.

Vocation has nothing to do with money, with career, with status, with ambition. I often see people corrode their vocation by insisting that it become a career — and then making career decisions that destroy their vocation. (Amy Winehouse's career destroyed her vocation, for instance.) The day that I feel my career is destroying my vocation, I will quit my career and go get a job, so that I can protect my vocation. But I will never quit my vocation. Nobody even needs to know about your vocation, in order for it to have meaning. Your vocation is holy because it has nothing to do with anyone else.

Your vocation can be anything that brings you to life and makes you feel like your soul is animated by purpose. Tending to your marriage can be your vocation. Raising your children can be your vocation. Teaching people how to take care of their health can be your vocation. Visiting your elderly neighbors can be your vocation. I have a friend who finds his vocation in picking up garbage off the streets wherever he goes; this is his gesture of love toward his fellow man. Searching for light and peace and meaning can be your vocation. Forgiveness can be your vocation.

Brother Lawrence was a 17th century monk who worked his whole life washing dishes in a monastery (because washing dishes was his JOB) but his vocation was to see God in everything and everyone, and that is why he radiated grace. (Awesome vocation, by the way. People came from all over the world to watch Brother Lawrence wash dishes, because of the way he radiated divine love in every act. THAT'S vocation.) I admire the Roman Catholic Church for understanding the sanctity of vocation, and for teaching that the purest human vocation is LOVE.

A vocation is the highest expression of your human purpose, and therefore you must approach it with deepest reverence. You can be called to your vocation by what you love (for instance: I love writing), or you can be called to your vocation by what you hate (for instance: I know people who dedicate themselves to social justice because of their hatred for violence and inequality.) If you don't have a vocation and you long for one, you can pray for one. You can ask the universe with humility to lead you to your vocation — but then you must pay VERY close attention to the clues and signs that point you toward your vocation. Don't just pray and WAIT. Instead, pray and SEEK.

Everyone wants the lightning strike, but the path to your vocation is usually a trail of bread crumbs, instead. Look for clues. No clue is too small; no vocation is insignificant. Don't be proud; be attentive. What brings your soul to life? What makes you feel like you are not just a meat puppet — not just here to work hard and pay bills and wait to die? You cannot be lazy or entitled about your vocation, or apathetic, or fatalistic, or calculating. You cannot give up on it, if things don't "work out" — whatever that even means. You must work closely with your intuition in order to find your highest meaning in life.

This is hard work sometimes, but it is divine work, and it is always worth it. (Here's a possibility, for instance: Searching for your vocation can be your vocation!) You can choose your hobbies, your jobs, or your careers, but you cannot choose your vocation; you can only accept the invitation that has been offered to you or decline it. You can honor your vocation, or you can neglect it. You can worship it, or you can ignore it. A vocation is offered to you as a sacred gift, and it is yours to care for, or to lose. When you treat your vocation as sacred, you will see your whole life as sacred — and everyone else's lives, too. When you are careless about your vocation, you will treat your whole life carelessly — and other people's lives, too. Your vocation will become clear to you through the act of PAYING ATTENTION to your senses and your soul, and to what in the world causes you to feel love or hate. You will be led to your vocation, though the path is not always obvious. You must participate in its unfolding. Do not fall asleep on this job. Your vocation is hinted at through your talents, tastes, passions, and curiosities.

Your vocation is calling you, even when you can't quite hear it. ("What you are seeking is seeking you" — Rumi.) When you embrace a vocation, and commit yourself to that vocation, your mind becomes a quieter place. When you accept the divine invitation of your vocation, you will become strong. You will know that — as long as you are tending to your vocation — everything will be fine.

My feeling is that people look for purpose in life without understanding these four words: HOBBY, JOB, CAREER, VOCATION. People blend these four concepts, or mistake them, confuse them, or try to have all four at once, or pretend that they are all the same thing. Or people just generally get freaked out and confused, because they haven't thought these words through, or decided which ones are most important. (Or which ones are most important RIGHT NOW.) People generally want to know, "What am I doing with my life?", but they don't slow down long enough to really think about these four different aspects of this question — the four different possibilities for where our time and energy goes. People worry so much about their careers, for instance, that they often forget to pay attention to their vocations. Or people get so seduced by the grandeur of their vocations that they forget to have a job, and so they stop taking care of themselves and their families in the material world...which will only bring suffering. (Remember: Even Brother Lawrence had a job. He was not too proud to wash dishes.) Or people are so busy chasing social status and personal advancement that they forget to make time for the relaxing joy of having a sweet little hobby. And oftentimes people mistake a sweet little hobby for something that they think should be a job, or a career, or a vocation. Don't try to blend what perhaps doesn't need to be blended. Don't mistake a job for a career, or a career for a vocation, or a vocation for a hobby, or a hobby for a job. Be clear about what each one is and be clear about what can be reasonably expected from each one and be clear about what is demanded of you with each one.

Here's another thing I see happening: people get so embarrassed or resentful about their lousy day jobs that they forget to be grateful that they have a job at all — and this causes only more anxiety and confusion, which again, will make them stop paying reverent attention to their vocation, or enjoying their hobbies, or making plans for a career.

We live in a real world that is heavy sometimes with real-life obligations, but we also have souls that deserve care and attention. We can pay attention to our worldly ambitions and pleasures (hobbies, jobs, careers) without neglecting our mystical, otherworldly, beautiful and often impractical vocations. We can pay attention to all of it — but this requires sitting still at times and really thinking things through, with courage and dignity. And it requires an understanding of terms.

The important thing is to be sober and careful and attentive enough to know what you are REALLY talking about when you consider the question, "What am I doing with my life?"

It isn't easy to answer this question but understanding and respecting these four different words might be a start.

And when in doubt, at least try SOMETHING. As the wonderful poet David Whyte says: "A wrong-headed but determined direction is better than none at all."

Good luck out there, brave seekers!

Onward,
LG"

Amazing, right?

It helped clarify so many things in my life. My purpose is creative expression. I am happiest and most alive when I am creating. Of course, I can do that in a variety of ways.

Your "job" and your "skillset" are not your purpose in life. Your purpose is to figure out what makes you come alive and then do more of that.

If you are stuck in a job you hate, you may believe you need to find a job that is your purpose.

No. You need to create a career path doing things you love that bring value to other people. Your purpose in the context of this book is to find more ways to have freedom, fulfillment, and flexibility. I believe deep down, we all want this.

We don't want to be hourly wage earners forever and have a deferred life.

We want to live life now…on our terms.

By reading this book, you are one step closer to your purpose because you are rejecting the status quo and searching for more meaning on your new career path.

This is a great image from this slideshare: https://www.slideshare.net/PuahHuiYing/finding-the-purpose-of-your-life-your-life-is-not-linear-66242182

Remember this: We stumble into clarity.

In my book, "How to Find Your Passion," I mention three tools that will help you tune in to your heart and to your soul:

- **Morning Pages (developed by author Julia Cameron, "The Artist's Way")**
- **The Artist Date (by Julia Cameron)**
- **Meditation**

We have followed the path of other people's expectations, our obligations, and society's definition of success. Now, it's time to live life on our terms.

For you, that may mean creating a small boutique business and working 3 hours a day, 4 days a week. Maybe for another person, it means being a subcontractor working for a few different people and supporting their business. Another person may decide it means getting a job in an industry that is growing and that supports their dreams and visions.

Whatever you choose, include your heart and soul.

I believe in YOU!

Chapter 8: Closing Thoughts

Now is a good time to reflect on these questions:

- What good is your career or job if it makes you miserable?
- What good is owning a beautiful house and furnishings if you are never home?
- What good is having great family, friends, and hobbies if you never have time to spend with them?

Are You Ready to Take Your Career and Financial Destiny Into Your Own Hands?

You are not a victim of the changes happening in the world. You have the power to shift and change directions.

Your career is your CREATION. You are the ARCHITECT of your career.

Plan, build, and strengthen your career so that you own it.

Commit to the following:

- **Look in the mirror**: Examine your curiosities, interests, values, priorities, and skills.
- **Look at others**: Uncover trends in the workplace, learn new skills, and find support. Think multiple career options.
- **Look forward**: The future is bright. Identify your goals, take action, and create your dream life.

Be an investigator and an experimenter. The great news is you don't have to get a two- or four-year degree at University only to discover that when you get "on the job," you hate it.

There are endless opportunities that require a small investment of your time, money, and energy. You can try doing new things and see if you enjoy doing them. You can't learn solely from reading a book. You must go out into the world and experiment.

You deserve to have meaningful work and a life on your terms. We all do.

Don't settle for less, and don't believe in the myth of instant satisfaction and instant answers.

Keep moving in the direction of what makes you come alive and what brings your heart and soul to life.

Thank you for taking the time to read this book, and I'm rooting for YOU!

Xxxxoooo,

Michelle

Notes

Notes

Notes

Notes

Notes

Notes

www.ingramcontent.com/pod-product-compliance
Lightning Source LLC
LaVergne TN
LVHW051848080426
835512LV00018B/3128